Where Are You Going?

Written by Professors
James Troy Chastain and Park Hye Jung

BAEKSAN Publishing Co

Preface

No matter where you are going, here is where you start.

If you interested in a carrier in the exciting Field of air travel or tourism. ***Where Are You Going*** is the resources you need packed with tourism English and industry language form real world professionals you'll be training for advancement in one of the largest businesses in world.

As a trained travel professional you can fit into this exciting growth industry.

The best part is that a full or part time travel career can be not only profitable but exciting and rewarding.

Work for a cruise line, airline, retailed travel agency, hotel resort, tour company, or corporation where you arrange and coordinate corporate travel needs.

Travel professionals enjoy a great variety of discounts on their personal travel. Airlines, cruise lines, tour companies, hotels and car rental agencies all offer special promotions and industry rates to their travel partners.

You can see and learn our exciting world, and you can get paid while you do it

항공기내, 공항, 호텔, 레스토랑 등 서비스현장에서 고객의 요구는 매우 다양하고, 발생 가능한 상황은 무수히 많습니다.

본서를 학습함으로 해서 그 모든 상황에 완벽히 대비할 수는 없겠지만, 실제 서비스현장에서 가장 활용도가 높은 서비스회화 표현들을 익힘으로써, 고객을 상대로 자신감 있고 즐거운 서비스가 가능할 것입니다.

모쪼록 본서가 멋진 서비스맨이 되기를 희망하는 모든 분들에게 도움이 되기를 바라며, 힘든 작업을 같이 해 온 제임스 교수님께 깊은 감사의 마음을 전합니다.

Contents

AIRLINE SERVICE

01 Chapter

Reservation Ticketing

Vocabulary

- reserve / reservation
- airline
- flight number
- round trip
- inbound / outbound
- ticket
- coach class
- schedule
- stopover
- overbooking
- confirm / reconfirm
- check-in
- address

Key Phrases

- Which airline would you prefer?

- What time would you prefer?

- When would you like to return?

- Would you like a round trip ticket?

- We have some seats available.

- May I have your name and telephone number, please?

- I'll check the schedule.

- The fare is $2,000.

- May I have your credit card and passport?

- Would you please sign here?

Warm up

Unscramble the sentences.

Your put I've stand-by list name

____

change you Would date flight departure like?

____

I many reserve may for How seats you?

____

for at It may 2:40 p.m. may for

____

I reserved flight 905 have flight, on June 25th. For your return

____

cancellation If to please contact make any changes or you want to your reservation, me anytime.

____

Dialogue

(A : Airline   P : Passenger)

Reservation

A : SEOUL Airlines. May I help you?

P : I'd like to make a reservation from Seoul to New York.

A : When would you like to leave, sir?

P : Any flights on November 22, on Saturday?

A : O.K. Saturday, November 22. We have some seats available.
We have two flights at 10 a.m. and 7 p.m.
What time would you prefer?

P : I'll take the 10 a.m. flight.

A : O.K. Would you like to book your return flight, too?

P : Yes. I'd like to return on December 7, Saturday.

A : December 7. Let me see.
Yes, we have some seats available at 11 a.m.
What class would you like- economy, business or first?

P : Economy class, please. What's the fare?

A : The Economy fare is $ 2,000 round-trip.

P : O.K. I'll take it.

A : Your name and phone number, please?

P : James Chastain, (010) 350-3500.

A : How do you spell your name?

P : J-A-M-E-S, C-H-A-S-T-A-I-N.

A : Yes, sir. Your reservation is made for Flight 026 leaving for New York on November 22, Saturday at 10 a.m.
Your reservation number is 350-3500.
Your return reservation on December 7, 11 a.m. is also confirmed.

You'll have to purchase your ticket at least three days before your departure.

P : I will. Thank you. Bye.

A : Thank you for calling. And have a nice day!

Ticketing

A : May I help you?

P : I want to purchase my ticket. I already have a reservation. My reservation number is 350-3500.

A : Your name, please?

P : James Chastain.

A : Yes, sir. 7 p.m. Saturday, SEOUL Airlines, right?

P : Right. How much is the fare?

A : It's $ 2,000 for round-trip.

P : Do you accept Visa card?

A : Sure. May I have your credit card and passport, please?

P : Here you are.

A : Would you sign here, please?

P : O.K.

A : Here is your ticket for New York, economy class, on Flight 028 leaving at 7 p.m. on November 22. Please be sure to check-in at the airport at least two hours before your flight. Anything else I can do for you?

P : No. Thanks.

A : You're welcome. Have a nice trip!

Other expressions

- Shall I make a reservation for you?

- Do you have a fixed date in mind?

- I am afraid we don’t have any direct flights to London.

- From Incheon to London, we have only one daily flight.

- I am afraid business class is fully booked.

- Would you like to take economy class?

- It still takes about 5 minutes to check.

- Your reservation is cancelled.

Exercise : Listening

Listen and fill in the blanks.

(A : Airline P : Passenger)

<u>Changing flight schedules.</u>

A : SEOUL Airlines. _______ ______ _______ ______?

P : Yes. I'd like to _________ ________ _________schedule.

A : _______ ________have your name?

P : James Chastain. And my _______ __ __________is 350-3500.

A : ________ ______________Mr. Chastain.

Your reservation is __________ ________ _________going to New York.

How would you like to change it?

P : I'd like ____________________afternoon flight.

A : Let ________________________there are any afternoon flights. Just a moment, please.

P : All right.

A : OK. We _________________________at 7 p.m.

P : Sounds great. I'll take it. ______me for the 7 p.m. flight, please.

A : All right, Mr. Chastain.
Your flight has been changed from ___________ __________ ____________________, leaving Incheon at 7 p.m. and arriving in New York is at 8 p.m.

P : Thank you so much.

A : You're __________ __________. Thank you for flying SEOUL Airlines.

Exercise

Create a dialogue using the prompts with a partner.

(A : Airline P : Passenger)

A : ________Airlines. May ____________________________?

P : I'd like to ____________________________?

A : When would you ____________________________?

P : ____________________________, on Saturday?

A : O.K. ____________________________. We have some seats available.

____

P : I'll ____________________________. flight.

A : O.K. Would you ____________________________?

P : Yes. ____________________________, Saturday.

A : ____________________________. Let me see.

____

What class would you like-

____________________________?

P : ____________________________?

A : ____________________________.

P : ____________________________.

A : ____________________________?

P : ____________________________ ____________________________.

A : How do you spell your name?

P : ____________________________ ________________________

A : Yes, sir. Your reservation ____________________________

____________________________.

Your reservation number is 350-3500.

Your return ____________________________is also confirmed.

You'll have to purchase your ticket at least three days before your departure.

P : ____________________________Thank you. Bye.

A : Thank you for calling. ____________________________day!

02 Chapter

Check-In

Vocabulary

- check-in
- carry-on baggage
- checked baggage
- excess baggage
- extra charge
- fragile
- baggage allowance
- baggage claim(tag)
- boarding pass
- window seat
- aisle seat
- unaccompanied child(minor)
- passport
- customs, immigration, quarantine
- transfer
- delay / hold-up

Key Phrases

- May I see your ticket and passport, please?

- Are you going to LA on flight 017?

- Do you have any baggage to check?

- How many pieces of baggage would you like to check?

- Could you put your baggage on the scale, please?

- Would you prefer a window seat or an aisle seat?

- The flight is scheduled to depart on time.

- Here are your baggage claim tag and boarding pass, sir.

- Have a pleasant flight.

Warm up

Unscramble the sentences.

Flight number your departure date May I have and, please?

boarding at and we expect is 2 to The gate begin about number 1:40.

on the put my list you Could name?

be on time sure to be Please.

our boarding Which is gate?

me to direct Gate Can you 7?

Dialogue

(A : Airline P : Passenger)

A : Good afternoon. What can I do for you, sir?

P : I want to check in, please. I'm going to New York on flight 028.

A : May I see your ticket and passport, please?

P : Here you are.

A : Are you going to New York on Flight 028?

P : That's right.

A : Do you have any baggage to check?

P : Just one. I'll carry this briefcase myself.

A : All right, sir. Anything breakable?

P : No.

A : Please put all carry-on luggage on the conveyor.

P : O.K.

A : Would you like a window seat or aisle seat?

P : I'd like an aisle seat, please.

A : Here are your boarding pass and baggage claim check. Your seat is 37C on the aisle. You'll be boarding at Gate number 13. Be sure to be on time.
Enjoy your trip, sir.

P : Thank you.

Other expressions

- We're sorry that our Flight 017 will be delayed due to dense fog(heavy snow, heavy rain, strong winds).
- The new arrival time will be 3:00 p.m.
- Further information will be announced as soon as possible.
- Please empty your pocket and go through again, sir.
- Boarding will start in a few minutes.

Exercise : Listening

Listen and fill in the blanks.

(A : Airline   P : Passenger)

A : Good morning. May I have your ________________ ______

____________, please?

P : I have _____ ______________

A : All right. I can find you on the computer.

Would you like an __________ ___________ or __________

____

P : Can I be assigned a seat by the ___________ ____________

_____________?

A : Yes, sir. But you may be asked to __________________________

________in the case of an emergency.

P : No problem.

A : All right. Do you have any ______________________________?

P : Just one.

A : Could you put your ____________ _____ ________ __________, please?

P : Sure.

A : Here are your boarding pass and ____________ __________ _________. ________________________. Boarding will begin at 9:30 a.m. Have a pleasant flight.

03 Chapter

Boarding Seating Guide

Vocabulary

- aboard
- boarding pass
- front
- back
- aisle
- empty seat
- occupied
- seating assignment
- upgrade
- seatbelt
- overhead bin
- inconvenience

Key Phrases

- May I see your boarding pass, please?

- Your seat is in the back of the cabin.

- Would you please take your seat during boarding?

- All the seats are occupied today.

- Would you please change seats?

- I'll check it for you right away.

- I'm sorry for the inconvenience.

Warm up

Unscramble the sentences.

1. there's my seat Excuse me, someone in.

2. you please boarding see your May I pass? Thank.

3. mistake in the seating I'm but I'm Come this way, please.

4. afraid there's sorry been a assignment.

5. I will here check Would this for you please wait for a moment? you right away.

6. waiting Thank sir for, you

7. seat reassigned has Your been.

Dialogue

(F : Flight Attendant P : Passenger)

Seating Guide

1.

F : Good morning, sir. Welcome aboard. May I see your boarding pass, please?

P : Good morning. Here you are.

F : Thank you. Your seat number is 58A in the back of the cabin. Straight to the back, please. You have a window seat.

P : Thank you.

F : You're welcome, sir.

2.

(passenger blocking the aisle / standing in the aisle)

F : Excuse me, sir. May I help you?

P : No. I'm just waiting for my friend.

F : Would you please take your seat during boarding?

P : OK, I'll sit.

F : Thank you, sir.

Changing Seats

P : Excuse me, my wife and I were assigned separate seats. Do you have any empty seats together?

F : I see, sir. Would you please wait until everyone has boarded, sir?
I'll check it for you right away.

1.

F : Thank you for waiting. We have some empty seats in the back of the cabin. Would that be alright, sir?

P : That'll be fine. Thank you.

F : Come this way, please.

2. (no seats available)

F : I'm sorry, sir. But all the seats are occupied today.
So I'll check if another passenger is willing to change his seat for you.

(go to P2)

F : Excuse me, sir. I'm sorry but we have a couple who has been assigned separate seats. Would you mind changing seats so they can sit together?

P : No, I don't. Where should I sit?

F : Thank you very much. And I'm sorry for the inconvenience, sir.
I'll show you where it is. This way, please.

Exercise : Listening

Listen and fill in the blanks.

(F : Flight Attendant　P : Passenger)

Wrong Seat

P1 : Excuse me, I think this is my seat.

F : ____________ ______________ ____________ __________ __________

____________, please?

Thank you.

(To P2)

________________, ma'am.

May I see your boarding pass, please?

________________, ma'am.

(to P2)

I'm________but I'm afraid you are in the ____________

______________yourseat is right behind this one.

P2 : All right. I'm sorry.

F : (to P2) ________________. May I help you with ____________

____________?

P2 : No, thank you.

F : (to P1) Thank you _________________________, sir. Here you are.

Other expressions

- May I help you find your seat?

- I'll show you to your seat. / I'll escort to your seat.

- Your seat is at the back of the opposite side.

- We have to re-check your boarding pass individually for your own security.

- Would you please change seats with that lady over there?

- Where would you like to sit?

- I'll see if it can be changed, sir.

- We can't upgrade passengers' seats.

- Is there anything else I can do for you?

- I'll ask one of our ground staff about that.

04 Chapter

Baggage Handling Prepapation For Take-Off

Vocabulary

- turbulence
- coatroom
- valuable
- emergency
- window shades
- bassinet
- bulkhead seat
- baby items
- delay / hold-up
- captain
- cockpit
- departure time
- destination
- lavatory
- upright
- recline

Key Phrases

- May I help you with your bag?

- Would you please keep your bag under the seat?

- It might fall out during the flight.

- We have to keep the aisle open.

- Would you care for a newspaper?

- I'll check if we have any left in the other galley.

Warm Up

Unscramble the sentences.

you your seat please belt Would fasten?

____

please your return Would upright position you seat to the?

____

please Would table you close your tray?

____

Mind your cellular turning Would you off phone?

____

shortly off We will taking be.

____

open Could your window you please shades?

____

Dialogue

(F : Flight Attendant P : Passenger)

Baggage Handling

F : Excuse me, ma'am. Is this your bag?

P : Yes, why?

F : Would you mind keeping your bag under the seat, please?
We must keep the aisle clear.

P : But my bag doesn't fit.

F : If you like, I'll be glad to keep it in the back of the cabin for you.

P : Oh, that's great. Thanks a lot.

F : It's my pleasure, ma'am.

Ground Service

F : Would you care for a newspaper, ma'am?

P : Do you have the Washington Post?

F : The Washington Post is not available on this flight.
Would you like the Korea Times instead while I check if we have any left in the other galley?

Preparation For Take-off

P : Can I use the lavatory now?

F : You can't use the lavatory during take-off.
We'll be taking off very soon.

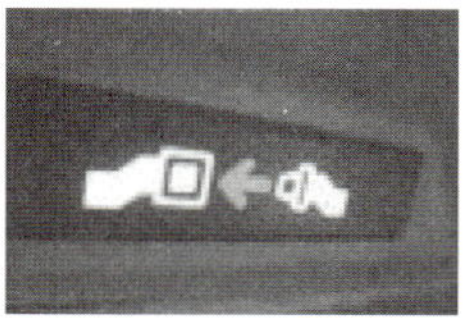

Delay

P : Why haven't we left yet?

F : We are waiting for connecting passengers.
We'll be taking off as soon as they arrive. Thank you for your patience.

Other expressions

- I'm sorry but I'm afraid you are not permitted to leave baggage here.

- All heavy or fragile items must be placed under your seat.

- Would you please keep your valuables with you?

- Our headsets are free of charge.

- If you need anything during the flight, please let us know.

- Would you please remain in your seat?

- Would you mind putting out your cigarette, please?

- I'm afraid the use of mobile phones is not allowed in the aircraft.

- I will get you a plastic bag filled with some ice cubes.

- You can put it in the bag and keep it with you.

- Would you please wait until after take-off?

Exercise : Listening

Listen and fill in the blanks.

(F : Flight Attendant　P : Passenger)

Mother With A Baby

F : Would you like to use a __________ for ________________?

P : I would be glad to.

F : I'll be back ______ ______ ______ a bassinet for your baby after take-off.

P : Thanks. Do you have ______________________ such as diapers?

F : Yes, we do, ma'am.

We have diapers, baby food, baby formula and bottles.

If you need anything for your baby, __________ __________ ________ ________.

P : All right. Thank you so much.

F : ________________, ma'am.

Would you please hold your baby ______________________?

That will be more comfortable and safer for the baby.

P : Oh, I see.

(After take-off)

F : Excuse me, ma'am.

__________ __________ ________me to set up a bassinet for you?

P : Yes, that'll be helpful.

F : There you are. ____________________________.

P : __________you _________much.

F : My pleasure. __________________________________.

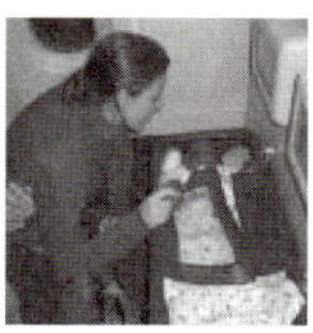

AIRLINE SERVICE

05 Chapter

In-Flight_meal Service

Vocabulary

- refreshing
- careful
- on board
- tray table
- chaser
- cocktail
- recommend
- entree
- run out of
- heat up
- special meal
- kosher meal

Key Phrases

Towel service

- Would you like to use a (refreshing / hot) towel?

- Please be careful. It's hot.

Beverage service

- Would you care for something to drink?

- What kind of juice would you like?

Meal service

- Would you please open your tray table?

- We have beef and Bi-Bim-Bap. Which would you prefer?

- We've run out of the beef today.

Warm Up

Unscramble the sentences.

1. right check I'll meal on your away.

2. I your you enjoy hope meal.

3. meal Are with you finished your?

4. scotch How you like would your?

5. instead you something like Would else?

Dialogue

(F : Flight Attendant P : Passenger)

Beverage service

1.

F : Would you like something to drink?

P : What kind of juice do you have?

F : We have orange, pineapple, tomato and guava juice, sir.

P : I'll have orange juice.

F : Certainly, sir.

2.

F : Would you care for something to drink before dinner?

P : Can I have some champagne?

F : I'm sorry, ma'am. Champagne is not served on this flight.
Would you like to drink something else?

P : Oh, I see. I'll have Scotch, then.

F : Certainly, sir. How would you like your Scotch?

P : I'd like Scotch & Soda, please.

F : Yes, sir. Would you like a chaser?

P : Just give me some water.

F : I see. Here you are. Enjoy your drink.

3. Refill

F : Would you like another cocktail, sir?

P : Yes, please.

F : What were you drinking, sir?

P : I had a Manhattan.

F : I see, sir. Just a moment, please.
Thank you for waiting, sir.
Here is your drink.

Service tips!

- Always smile and eye contact when you talk with passengers.
- Call passengers by their name even when you answer to them.
  "Certainly, Mr. Chastain."
- Try to reply with more than one word.
  "Yes, I'll bring you a Gin & Tonic right away, Mr. Chastain."
- Induce the conversation rather than waiting for a request.
  "Is everything alright, Mr. Chastain?"
- Be diligent in making a reply and expressing your feelings.
  "Oh, did you? I'm glad to hear that!"
- Say sincerely that you're sorry for the matter.
  "I'm sorry for the inconvenience, Mr. Chastain."
- Explain understandable circumstances.
  "We are waiting for the clearance from the control tower."
- Propose alternative choices to the passenger.
  "Could I get you something else, instead?"

Meal service

1.

F : Excuse me, ma'am. Would you like to have lunch?

P : Yes, please.

F : Would you please open your tray table?
We have a choice of beef steak and chicken with sour sauce for dinner.
Which one would you prefer?

P : I'd like beef.

F : I am sorry, sir. But I'm afraid We are all out of beef just now,
But we have chicken. Would that be alright?

P : I'm sorry but I'm allergic to chicken. Do you have anything else?

F : I see, sir. I'll check whether we have anything else to offer for you.

2. Korean dish (Bi-Bim-Bap)

F : We have a choice of a Korean dish or a Western dish.
Which would you prefer?

P : What is the Korean dish?

F : It is called Bi-Bim-Bap, a traditional Korean dish.
It is rice, vegetables, sesame oil, and hot pepper paste mixed together.
If you don't like spicy food, you can eat it without the hot pepper paste.
You can enjoy it by mixing ingredients together.

P : Okay. I'll try that.

F : Hear you are. Enjoy your meal.

How to enjoy "BIBIMBAP" (韓式拌飯)
ビビンバの召し上がり方
Comment manger le "BIBIMBAP"

VACUUM-PACKED STEAMED RICE
真空パックのご飯
RIZ VAPEUR EN SOUS VIDE

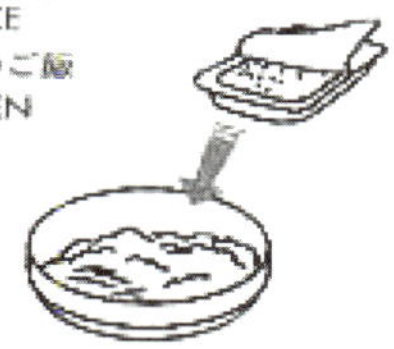

1. Put the steamed rice into the BIBIMBAP bowl.

   ご飯を器に入れます。

   Versez le riz vapeur dans le bol à BIBIMBAP

TUBE OF KOREAN HOT PEPPER PASTE
コチュジャン（唐辛子味噌）
TUBE DE PÂTE DE PIMENT

SESAME OIL
ごま油
HUILE DE SÉSAME

2. Add the sesame oil and hot pepper paste as you want. The paste might be spicy.

   お好みに合わせて
   コチュジャンとごま油を入れて
   お召し上がりください。

   Ajoutez l'huile de sésame et la pâte de piment selon votre propre goût. Cette dernière pouvant être épicée.

3. Mix the ingredients well

   よく混ぜます。

   Mélangez bien tous les ingrédients

SIDE DISH
サイドディッシュ
ACCOMPAGNEMENT

SOUP
スープ
SOUPE

4. Soup and side dish are included with your BIBIMBAP dish.

   わかめスープとサイドディッシュと
   いっしょにお召し上がりください。

   La soupe et l'accompagnement sont inclus dans votre plat de BIBIMBAP.

3. Special meal

F : Excuse me, sir.

Did you request a Kosher meal?

P : Yes, I did.

F : Here is your meal.

May I unwrap your meal box and heat it up for you?

P : Yes, please.

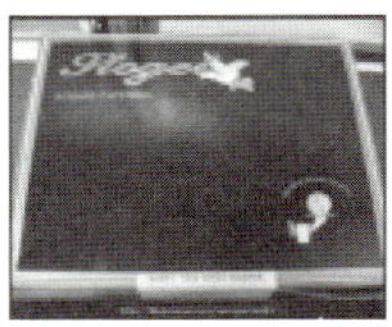

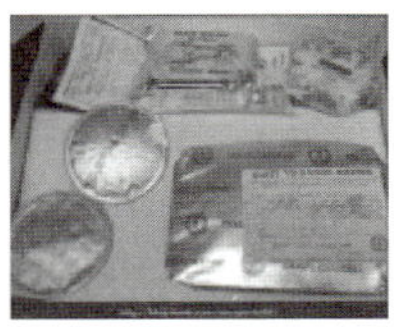

4. Coffee and Tea Service

F : Would you care for some coffee?

P : Yes, please.

F : May I have your cup, please?
Here you are. Would you like cream and sugar?

P : Thank you.

F : Would you care for a cup of tea?

P : Yes, please.

F : Here you are.
Would you like some lemon with your tea?

P : Yes, please.
And my wife wants coffee.

F : Another cabin attendant will be here with coffee, sir.
(Another attendant will be along with coffee.)
Just a moment, please.

Other Expressions

- I'm sorry, sir. I'm afraid we cant make a Manhattan on board.

- May I put some ice in it?

- Excuse me, the cart is passing through. Please watch out (your knees)!

- May I take away your glass?

- Did you have a nice rest? Would you like a drink before breakfast?

- Did you order vegetarian meal?

- I'll get your meal for you as soon as possible.

- Here is your seaweed soup. Be careful, it's hot.

- Please give me your tray and keep your cup.

Exercise : Listening

Listen and fill in the blanks.

(F : Flight Attendant P : Passenger)

P : I'll have a ________________________.

F : I'm ________ _________ __________ that drink. Could you tell me how it's made?

P : It is made of __________ juice, ___________ and _____________.

F : I'm _________, sir. But we don't have peach tree ________ _________. Would you like ___________ __________, instead?

P : What do you __________?

F : May I suggest you try ____________ & ____________?

P : I'll try that.

F : Here you are__________________________________it.

P : ______________very much.

F : Would you like _________________?

P : Yes. Can I have __________________?

F : __________________. Here you are.

06 Chapter

Other In-Flight Services

Vocabulary

- entry card
- disembarkation card
- embarkation card
- customs form
- quarantine form
- purser
- arrival time
- declare
- declaration form
- citizen / resident
- fill out / complete
- method of payment

Key Phrases

- Would you please fill out these forms before we get to Seoul?

- One customs form is enough for each family.

- You have to declare any valuables that you have on the other side.

- Would you like to buy any duty-free items?

- They are all sold out. / We have run out of ○○○ now.

- Do you have any other currency instead?

- We will be starting the movie shortly.

- Would you please close the window shade?

Warm up

Unscramble the sentences.

Hope movie you I enjoy the.

All Customs form entering Korea must fill passengers out the.

Dollars pay won in Will you U.S or Korean?

Both sides You must form fill out of the.

I'll get I need for you right copy of the entry form another one away.

Dialogue

(F : Flight Attendant P : Passenger)

Distribution of Entry Document

P : Excuse me, I'm a tourist. Do I need this card?

F : Yes, sir. All passengers entering Korea must fill out the immigration form.

P : I see. Do you have an English form?

F : Yes, sir. I'll get one for you right away.
Here you are, sir.

F : Do you have anything to declare?

P : No, I don't have anything to declare.

F : Do you have more than 10,000 U.S dollars?

P : No.

F : Do you have any plants or meats?

P : No, I don't.

Transit Passenger

1.

F : Would you please fill out these forms before we get to Seoul?

P : I'm a transit passenger. I just change planes at Incheon.
I'm staying at the airport. Do I need these cards?

F : No, sir. You don't need to fill out these cards.

2.

F : Excuse me, sir. Where is your final destination?

P : I'm going to Sydney tonight.

F : Are you planning to stay at the airport or check in to a hotel in Seoul?

P : I'm going to take a half-day tour in Seoul.

F : Then, please fill out these forms, sir. These are the entry and customs forms.

- What's the purpose of your trip?
- May I have your telephone number in the U.S?
- May I ask where you will be staying in London?
- How long are you going to stay in Seoul?
- Are you carrying $10,000 or more with you?
- Do you have more than $10,000 with you?
- Do you have any plants or fruit with you?
- Do you have anything to declare?
- Are you a U.S citizen or a resident?
- Are you a resident or a visitor?
- Do you have an alien registration card?
- Do you have a green card?
- Are you traveling for business or pleasure?

Group / Family

P : I'm traveling in a group. Should each of us fill out this entry form?

F : Yes, sir. Each passenger must fill out the entry card separately.

P : I'm traveling with my family. Should each of us fill out this customs form?

F : Each passenger is required to complete an entry card. But one customs form is enough for each family.
If you are a family, just fill out one sheet.

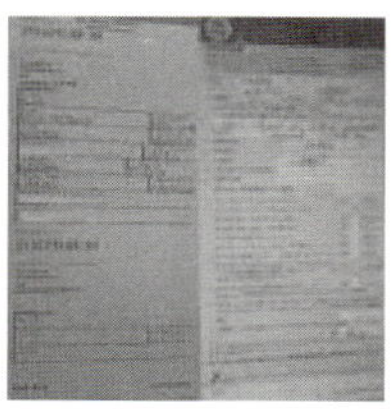

Duty Free Sales

1.

F : Would you like to buy any duty-free items?

P : What kind of duty-free items do you have?
I'd like to buy some cigarettes. What kind of cigarettes do you have?

F : Here is a shopping guide, sir. It will show you the selections we have.
We have Marlboro, Mild Seven, and some others, sir.

P : How much are they?

F : Most cigarettes are 15 dollars a carton and Korean cigarettes are 13 dollars a carton.

P : Could I have two cartons of Marlboro?

F : Sure. Here you are. The total comes to 30 dollars. How would like to pay?

P : Can I pay with my credit card?

F : Yes, sir. Would you please sign here?

2. Acceptable Currency

F : Here you are. 40 dollars altogether, sir?

P : I don't have any dollars. Do you accept Thailand Baht?

F : I'm sorry, sir. I am afraid we don't accept Thailand Baht.
Do you have any other currency?

P : I have some Japanese Yen.

F : That'll be fine, sir.

Movie

1.

P : Miss, when are you showing the movie?

F : Right after the in-flight sales, sir.
It will begin in about one hour from now.

P : What is the title of today's movie?

F : Today's movie is 'Silk Road'.

P : Oh, I see.

F : Our in-flight magazine has more detailed information about our movies.

2.

P : I don't think my earphones are working.

F : Let me check it for you, sir.
Alright, I will bring another headset for you. Just a moment, please.

F : Here you are. Can you hear now?

P : No, nothing at all.

F : I'm afraid the sound system in this seat is out of order.
I'll check if we have any empty seats available.
Just a moment, please.
We have an empty seat in the front of the cabin.
Would you like to move to that seat?

Other expressions

- Each passenger entering the United States must complete the document.

- Even if you have nothing to declare, you need to fill out the customs form.

- We take Korean Won, U.S Dollar, Japanese Yen, European Euro.

- So you know how much perfume I can take into Hong Kong?

- This magazine has more detailed information on our movie program.

- In-flight movie is not played for this flight.

Exercise : Listening

Listen and fill in the blanks.

(F : Flight Attendant P : Passenger)

U.S Citizen or Resident / Canadian Citizen

F : ___________, ma'am. Are you ___ __________ _________ or a resident?

P : Yes, I'm a ________citizen.

F : Then you don't need this entry card, but you must fill out the customs form.

Exercise : Speaking Activity

Create a dialogue using the prompts with a partner.

(F : Flight Attendant　P : Passenger)

P : How many ______________ _______ whiskey can I bring into Korea?

F : ______________ bottle ________________ tax-free, sir.

P : ________________ _______________ cigarettes?

F : _____________________________ is allowed tax-free.

P : I see. Then I will buy _________ ____________ of Marlboro and __________ bottle of Johnnie Walker.

F : Yes, sir. Here you are.
Would you prefer U.S Dollars or Korea Won, sir?

P : What is the exchange rate?

F : The exchange rate ________________________________.

P : Then I will _________________________they?

F : _________________dollars altogether, sir.

P : All I _________________. Do you have change?

F : Yes, sir. Here is your change, _____________________.

07 Chapter

Passenger Care Preparation For Landing

Vocabulary

- complimentary copy
- souvenir
- flying time
- delay
- turbulence
- airsickness (bag)
- chilly
- dizzy
- upset stomach
- a sore throat
- parking area
- slippery
- watch your step
- windy
- wet

Key Phrases

- Do you feel better now? / How are you feeling now?
- Do you have any medicine for headache?
- We are beginning preparation for landing.
- Would you please close your tray table?
- We'll be landing shortly.
- Could you please remain seated until the plane comes to a complete stop?
- We've not reached the parking area yet.
- I hope to see you on board again soon.

Warm up

Unscramble the sentences.

Good bye and have a nice stay in Seoul.

landing you please keep seat until Would after your bag under the?

position you seat please landing return Could your to the upright for?

indigestion have anythingheartburn I and, do you have?

Dialogue

(F : Flight Attendant P : Passenger)

General Questions

1.

P : Miss, how do I recline my seat?

F : Just push this button and lean back, sir.
Are you enjoying the flight?

P : Yes, it's alright.

F : Would you like a newspaper or a magazine?

P : No, thanks. I already have one.

F : Would you care for something to drink?

P : Coffee, please.

F : Certainly, sir. I'll get some for you right away.

2.

P : Miss, can I take this In-flight magazine?

F : Certainly, sir. It's your complimentary copy.

P : Can I take this earphone set as a souvenir?

F : I'm sorry, but they should be left on board.

Arrival Time

P : Excuse me. How long will it be before we get to New York?

F : We expect to arrive in about one hour and thirty minutes from now.

We'll be landing at about 10 a.m. local time.

Stopover

P : How long are we going to be on the ground in Anchorage?

F : About an hour, sir.

P : Can I remain in the cabin?

F : We need all the passengers to depart the plane so that we can clean the cabin. You might enjoy looking around at the airport.

P : Can I leave my bag here?

F : I'm afraid not, sir.
Would you please keep it with you when you depart the plane?

P : OK.

Other expressions

- I'm sorry, but I'm afraid there are no sleepers ready in Economy class.

- I'm afraid you might hear the noise from the galley.

- Would you like to use this slumber mask to help you sleep?

- Would you like a blanket and pillow?

- May I have your earphone set, please?

- Is your seatbelt fastened?

- I'm sorry to disturb you, but may I take down the bassinet now?

- We'll be landing very soon and the bar has closed.

- We've stopped the drink service for landing.

- What's the weather like in Seoul?

Exercise : Listening

Listen and fill in the blanks.

(F : Flight Attendant　P : Passenger)

Farewell Greeting

(A passenger is taking out the baggage from the overhead bin during taxiing)

F : ____________me, sir.

We've not ____________ ____________ ____________area yet.

____________ ____________ ____________ ____________until the plane comes to a complete stop?

P : Alight.

F : ________ ________.

Exercise

Create your own farewell greeting be creative and professional

HOTEL SERVICE

H O T E L   S E R V I C E

08 Chapter

Hotel Service Reservation

Vocabulary

- reservation
- turn down service
- single
- double
- suite
- bell man
- fully booked
- concierge
- pick up service
- key card
- laundry service
- wake up call
- room service
- service charge
- continental breakfast

Key Phrases

- I'm sorry sir, we're fully booked.

- Here is your key card.

- We offer free pick up service.

- All our rooms include the continental breakfast.

- I'll have the Bell man help you with your baggage.

- The only room still left is on the third floor. Will that do?

- I am sure you will find everything satisfactory. If you need anything, please call us.

- Taxis are hard to get at this time of the day. Can I call one for you?

- According to my present plan, I'll be checking out Wednesday morning.

Dialogue

(C : Clerk　T : Traveler)

1.

C : Good afternoon, sir. May I help you?

T : Yes, please. Do you have a double room available for four nights from tonight?

C : Just a moment, sir. I'll check it. ......
Yes, we do.

T : What's your rate per night?

C : 250 dollars plus tax.

T : Okay. I'll take it. I want a quiet room with a good view.

C : We have a room on the 9th floor facing the ocean. I'd like to recommend room 903, if you want.

T : That'll be fine. Does your rate include breakfast?

C : No, sir. May I see your passport, please?

T : Yes. Here you are.

C : Would you fill out this registration form, please?

T : Sure.

C : Can you just check through the details before signing here?

2.

C : Thanks for calling the park hotel.
How can I help you?

T : I need a room tonight.

C : Do you have a reservation?

T : No, I don't.

C : Ok. Let me check. ......
Well, you're in luck we have a single open. Will that be ok?

T : Sure. That's fine. Oh, could I get a wake up call for 6 a.m.?

C : Certainly sir. Wake up call 6 a.m. Also all ours rooms include the continental breakfast.

T : That's great. What are the room rates?

C : Single for one night is $85. How would you like to pay?

T : Do you take visa?

C : We certainly do sir. Here is your key card. Your room is on the

7th floor room 702.

T : Great thanks.

C : Have a great night. Thank you for choosing the park.

Exercise : Listening

Listen and fill in the blanks.

1. Of course. We offer turn ________ ________ as well as ________ service from the ________ free of charge.

2. I'm sorry sir. We are ________ ________. I can ________ ________ hotel and see if they have any rooms available.

3. Can I get a 6:30 a.m. ____________________?

4. Seoul has a number of tourist attractions checks with ________ ______________ see what other services are available.

5. I need any suit ________. Do you offer a ______________.

6. Hi. is this ________ ________ I would like a ________ ________ ________ sent to room 301 please.

7. Well, a ________ ________ ______ ______. But if you really want comfort I would suggest the presidential suite.

8. I'm sorry. We don't have a suite left. But I can offer a ______ ____________with two beds.

9. Your room is ______ ______ ______ _____key card. Would you like a wake up call?

10. There is a ______ ______ ______10% for ______ ______ ______ or more.

Exercise

Exercise Reservation dialogue form.

A) good morning. thanks for calling the double tree high land resort. How can I help you?

B) Yes. I need to make a reservation.

A) Ok, sir. Can I get your name please?

B) Yes. its Mr. Noris , Chuck Noris.

A) Ok, Mr. Noris and when will you be joining us?

B) On June 24 until June 28.

A) Very good sir. And what kind of room would you like?

B) The presidential suite of course.

A) Very well. Is there anything else I can help you with?

B) No that should take care of it.

A) Excellent, sir. Your total is 675$ that would be for 4 night stay in the presidential suite. How will you be paying?

B) Chuck Noris, only pays cash.

A) Very well sir. We look forward to seeing you on June 24th.

ROOM NO.	RATE

MAY WE RESERVE A ROOM AHEND FOR YOU?

YES____ NO____

IF YES, NAME

____

____

AT OUR HOTEL IN:

CITY ____________

ADRESS ____________

STATE ____________

ARRIVING ____________

DEPARTING ____________

ROOM NO.		CEPART DATE	RATE

PLEASE PRINT

LAST NAME　FIRST　NTIAL

NO IN PARTY

HOME ADDRESS

STREET

CITY　STATE　ZIP

COMPANY ADDRESS

STREET

CITY　STATE　ZIP

YEARMAKE OF CAR	LICENSE PLATE#	STATE

METHOD OF PAYMENT:

☐ CASH　☐ CHECX

☐ CREDIT CARD　NAME ____________

SIGNATURE

CLERK'S INITIAL　TIME CHECKED IN

#678901 *Gracious International Inns*

HOTEL SERVICE

09 Chapter

Room Service

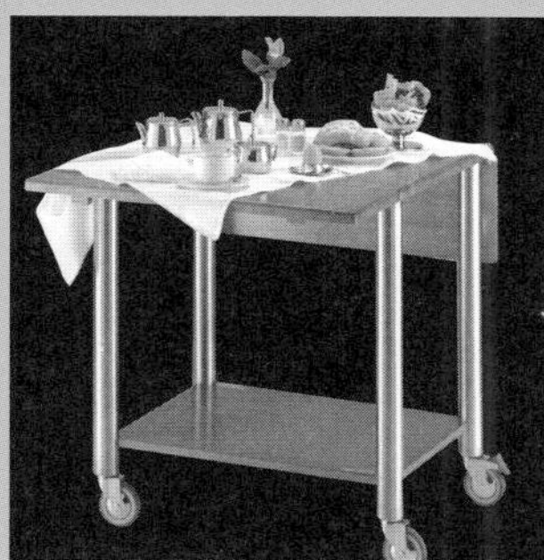

Vocabulary

- over-easy-medium-hard
- omelet
- hash browns
- brunch
- charge room
- cart
- wrap
- caviar
- champagne
- espresso
- appetizers
- poached

Key Phrases

- We offer Espresso / orange juice / mineral water / hot tea with the continental breakfast
- I'm in room 707 / 1615......
- How would you like you eggs cooked?
- I'd like them poached / sunny-side up / over-easy / scrambled
- What time would you like breakfast?
- Please, bring it at 8:30 / 7:00
- Would you like hash browns with that?
- Ok, wrap the Valentine's Day special and put it on the cart.

Warm up

Unscramble the sentences.

Good, room help service, may I afternoon you

____

Some I spaghetti like to order I with meat would sauce.

____

drink with that sir anything to

____

I'll coke yes take a

____

Taylor Very coke to room 1245good with meat sauce and Mr. spaghetti a

____

Dialogue

(R : Room Service G : Guest)

1.

R : Good morning, room service. May I help you?

G : Hello, We want to have a continental breakfast for two.

R : Very well, sir. Which juice would you like, tomato or orange?

G : One orange and one tomato.

R : All right, sir. Would you care for coffee or tea?

G : Bring us coffee, please.

R : Very well, sir. May I have your name and room number, please?

G : This is Mr. Miller. Room 1170.

2.

G : This is Mr. Harris in room 1435. Do you have a bottle of champagne in an ice bucket?

R : Yes, we do, sir. Any other drinks or some side dishes?

G : Oh, yes. What brands of scotch do you have?

R : We have many, sir. We recommend Knight Scotch.

G : Okay, one bottle of Knight Scotch. For some appetizers bring us smoked salmon, caviar and French fries. Oh, yes. Get a few bottles of club soda, too.

Exercise : Speaking activities

A. Make sentences out of the words below.

1. Could / room number / have / your / I / please?

2. How / would / your eggs / like / you / done?

3. I'd / poached / them / like / please.

4. What time / would / your breakfast / like / you / served

B. Fill in the blanks and practice the completed dialog with your partner.

(R : Room Service G : Guest)

R : Hello, room service. How may I help you?

G : Yes, I would like to order breakfast for tomorrow.

R : What time ____________?

G : At 8:30, please.

R : And what ____________?

G : I'd like two eggs on toast, please.

R : How would ____________?

G : Scrambled, please.

R : And would you ____________ with that?

G : I'll have an orange juice, please.

C. Match each question with the appropriate response.

1. What time would you like your breakfast served?

2. How would you like your eggs done?

3. What would you like to drink?

4. Could I have your room number, please?

A. I'm in room 707.

B. Espresso, please.

C. I'd like them poached.

D. Please, bring it at 8:30.

Exercise : Listening

Listen and fill in the blanks.

A) Good ____________ ____________ __________ how can I help you?

B) Yes, I would like the _____________ ____________ __________ _________, sent to my room.

A) Ok sir _________________________________ like that cooked?

B) ____________ __________, please and could also send a dozen red roses with that.

A) Ok sir Valentine's Day __________ for two and a dozen red roses, anything to drink.

B) What red wine ______________________________?

A) We have a ___________ _________ _______ that goes great with the beef.

B) Ok that sounds great.

A) Ok that a Valentine's Day special one house burgundy and a dozen red roses, would like us to ___________ ___________ _________?

B) That would be great.

A) What room shall I send it to?

B) I'm in 1503.

A) Very well sir. ______________________________.

10 Chapter

Hotel Tourist Services

Vocabulary

- retail
- travel
- compact / mid / full size
- mileage
- gift
- across from
- next to
- concierge
- intersection
- rotary

Key Phrases

- Yes, sir. The cost of the room includes the complimentary continental breakfast.

- The museum is across from the city park and next to the library.

- The concierge desk offers a full line of services to help travelers.

- $19.90 a day including 500 miles, plus mileage.

- I want to rent a compact size car.

- Do you want to purchase travelers insurance?

Exercise

Match each question with the appropriate response.

1. Are you here on your honeymoon?

2. What time does the next tour leave?

3. How much does this shirt cost?

4. Can I get one in a larger size?

5. Do you take Canadian dollars?

6. Would you gift-wrap this, please?

A. the next one is at 2:30.

B. certainly, let me get one for you.

C. yes, we do.

D. no, we just drove up for the weekend.

E. we can do that here.

F. it costs $12.99.

Exercise : Listening

Listen and fill in the blanks.

(S : Concierge Service C : Customer)

S : May I help you, sir?

C : Yes, please. I want to take a ______ ___ ____ _____ _____. I need to find something for my kids.

S : that would be on the third floor _______ ____ ______ _______, they have a wonderful selection of toys and gifts for kids.

C : _____________the escalator?

S : Just ahead. Right past the ________ ______on the left.

C : ________ _______.

Exercise : Speaking activities

A : Match each question with the appropriate response.

Ground transportation

1. Can you tell me where the limousine leaves?

____

2. How is the traffic today?

____

3. Where are you going today?

____

A. it is very slow.

B. to the park hotel, please.

C. the limousines leave just over there.

B : Fill in the blanks and practice with a partner.

(T : tourist D : driver)

D : Where ________________ today, sir?

T : Could you ________ ________ ________

________ ______, please.

D : ____________, sir. Where are you from, if you don't mindme asking?

T : I'm Korean. I've ________ ________ ________

____________. Have you ever visited Korea before?

D : No, ________ ________ ________ to go one day. Is this your first time in ________?

T : No, I've been here ________ ________ before on holiday. Could you tell me how the traffic is at the moment?

T : Well, it's still early. So the ________________________

________. It should make for easy traveling.

T : Great

C. Put the following sentences in the correct order to make a conversation between a tourist and a driver. Role-play the dialog with your partner.

(T : tourist D : driver)

D : Well, it's very slow.

T : Could you tell me how traffic is at the moment?

D : No problem, sir.

T : Could you take me to the park hotel, please?

D : Where are you going today, sir?

D. Makesentences out of the words below.

1. What kind / you / do / of car / want?

2. Would / insurance / like / you / with that?

3. What / have / you / do / available?

4. Can / a car / I / rent / for three days?

E. Fill in the blanks and practice the completed dialog with your partner.

(C : clerk T : tourist)

C : May I help you?

T : Good morning. Can _______for three days?

C : Sure, when do you want to pick it up?

T : Nine a.m. Tuesday.

C : What kind of car do you want?

T : I'd like _______. What's the rate?

C : $19.90 a day including 500 miles, plus 50 cents per mile.

T : I'll take it.

C : How will you be paying, sir?

T : Here _______.

C : The car will be ready for you in the parking lot tomorrow.

T : Can I drop _______.

C : Certainly, sir. By 9 a.m. Friday morning, make sure you fill her up. Just leave the key in the car and lock it.

Dialogue

1.

(T : tourist D : driver)

D : Where are you going today, sir?

T : Could you take me to the park hotel, please.

D : No problem, sir. Where are you from, if you don't mind me asking?

T : I'm Korean. I've just arrived here from Seoul. Have you ever visited Korea before?

D : No, but I'd love to go one day. Is this your first time in England?

T : No, I've been here several timesbefore on holiday. Could you tell me how the traffic is at the moment?

T : Well, it's still early. So the traffic is not too bad. It should make for easy traveling.

T : Great

2.

(T : tourist C : clerk)

T : I want to rent a mid -size car for three days, please.

C : Our rate is $36.99 with insurance.

T : That's fine.

C : Can I have your driver's license, credit card and passport, please.

T : Here they are.

C : And you stay here in town?

T : I'm staying at the comfort inn.

C : Sign here, sir.

T : Do you have a Map?

C : There is already one in the car.

T : Good.

C : Here are the keys. Have a good trip.

Exercise : Activity

Person 1 : Look at the map from the last activity and write direction to the places listed below.

Hotel	
Police station	
School	
Car center	

Person2 : Practice asking question about the location and giving directions.

Person3 : Work in partners, each partner chooses a different location on the map. Partner A will then give that location to partner B who will write the directions to that location.

Then practice dialogues similar to those in the examples.

Person1 : Excuse me, where is the ________.

Person2 : Go ___________________________.

___________________________.

Person1 : Thank you

Person2 : You're welcome.

rooftop	Sky park
5th floor	Restaurant
4th floor	Fitness center
3rd floor	Currency Exchange
2nd floor	Coffee shop
1st floor	Payphones
basement	Parking lot

In groups of two, take turns asking each other where different facilities are located within the hotel.

Example :

Excuse me, where is the swimming pool?

It's on the rooftop.

Dialogues

1.

Person1 : Excuse me, can you tell me where the restaurant is?

Person2 : Sure, go straight for two blocks and right at the intersection. Keep going straight past the police station and it will be on your right. You can't miss it.

Person1 : Great, thank you.

2.

Person 1 : Excuse me, can you tell me where the photo shop is?

Person2 : Certainly, go straight for one block and turn right at the first intersection. Keep going straight to the next intersection and turn left. It will be on your right, across from the post office.

Person1 : Thank you so much.

Other expressions

- We have both compact and mid-size.

- Just put it on my credit card.

- Certainly, sir.

- No, I don't want to pay the extra cost.

- Our special is $29.99.

- Here you go.

- I'd like a van.

11 Chapter

Hotel Resort Food & Beverage Front of the House

Vocabulary

- back waiter
- run
- window
- garnish
- rare, medium, well
- hostess station / map
- wait station
- dressing
- 10, 8, 2 top
- grilled
- specials
- soup of the day
- dessert tray

Key Phrases

- How would you like that cooked?

- What kind of dressing would you like?

- Any sides with that.

- We have an 8 top coming in at 8'oclock.

- Please present the dessert tray to table 12 after it is garnished.

- Do you want that straight up or on the rocks.

Dialogue

Taking a Reservation

Hostess : Thanks for calling the bungalow. How can I help you?

Guest : I'd like to make a reservation for tonight.

Hostess : Ok. What time?

Guest : 7 o'clock for 5 people.

Hostess : Ok. Can I have your name?

Guest : Yes. It's Patrick Cornwall. It's my wife's Birthday so make it a nice table.

Hostess : Yes, sir. Thanks for calling. See you at 7.

Table service

Hostess : Hi, Welcome to the Bungalow. Three for dinner, come this way please. Here's our menu our special today is Pecan crusted sea bass in an orange butter sauce. Your server will be right with you.

Server : Hello, everyone. Can I start you off with something to drink or an appetizer?

Guest1 : Yes, I like a house wine.

Guest2 : Water is fine for me.

Guest3 : I'll take a coke please.

Server : Ok. A coke, a house wine and water for you. Would you like to order or do you need more time?

Guest1 : I think we're Ready, I'll have the New York strip cooked very rare with the grilled asparagus and new potatoes.

Server : Excellent.

Guest2 : And I'll try the sea bass special.

Guest3 : I think I'll go for the grilled chicken Caesar.

Server : Wonderful. Then that's a New York cooked rare, one special and a chicken Caesar salad, anything else?

Guest3 : No, that's all.

Server : Great. I get these right back to you.

Homemade Soups

Made-from-scratch daily!

Cup *4.95*

Bowl *6.95*

Chicken Caesar Salad

Grilled or blackened chicken, crisp romaine tossed
with aged parmesan, herb-garlic
Croutons and creamy Caesar dressing *9.25*

Starters

Spinach Artichoke Dip

Blended with aged parmesan and slow baked.
Served with and garlic toast *9.95*

California Chicken Quesadilla

Grilled corn tortillas filled with chicken, jack & cheddar cheese,
fresh avocado, green onions, mild *11.95*

From the Grill

New York Steak

12oz Choice center-cut char-grilled to perfection server with roasted
vegetables and loaded baked potato *25.95*

Steak (Top Sirloin) & Lobster

7oz Certified USDA Prime Top Sirloin aged 28 to 35 days then seasoned, char-grilled to perfection and served with a premium 8oz Lobster Tail ····· 36.95

From the sea

Grilled Salmon

Our Salmon is flame grilled and brushed with garlic herb butter. Served with roasted vegetables and one side choice. ····· 20.95

Pasta

Chicken & Broccoli Alfredo

Grilled chicken, fresh broccoli and egg & spinach noodles with creamy Alfredo sauce ····· 13.95

Side orders

Fresh Grilled Asparagus (Seasonal) ····· 4.75

Baked Sweet Potato ····· 5.50

Roasted Vegetables ····· 4.75

Loaded Baked Potato ····· 5.00

Beverages

House wine (Chablis) ····· 6.75

Pint of draft beer (soft drinks) ····· 5.75

Cola sprite fanta ····· 3.75

Exercise

Create a dialogue.

For a four top order from the menu

GUEST CHECK

Date	Table	Guests	Server	No 1198626

APPT-SOUP/SAL-ENTREE-VEG/POT-DESSERT-BEV

		Tax		
		Thank You Total		

BTGC-525

Date	Amount	Guests	No 1198626

1		
2		
3		
4		
5		
6		
7		
8		
9		
10		
11		
12		
13		
14		
15		
16		
17		
18		
Transfor to front Total		

Thank you!

Server suport dialogues

Server's job is communication not only with the guest but the whole staff from the bartenders, the hostess, back waiters and the cooks.
Efficient service can be complete until all parts of the restaurant runs smoothly.

1. Server Hostess

Server : Have you seated table 27 yet?

Hostess : Let's check the map. No I'm sorry. It's reserved at 7:30.

Server : Ok. That's not too far off, I you see the back waiter have him water my whole section. I'm really busy!

Hostess : Ok. I see if I can find him.

Server : Thanks.

2. Bar / Server

(B/T : Bartender)

Server : Ok. I need cosmopolitan, bourbon on the rocks, and a Shirley temple.

B/T : Ok. Coming up. The cosmopolitan is in the bucket.

Server : Does the bourbon get a garnish?

B/T : No. but the cosmopolitan get an orange slice and a cherry and the Shirley temple gets a cherry.

Server : Thanks.

3. Back Waiter / Server

Back waiter : Have you been to table 28 yet?

Server : No not yet.

Back waiter : Ok I just watered them but they look like their in a hurry.

Server : Ok, thanks clean up 25 and ill get to them. Also bring 27 more bread.

Back waiter : You want more bread to 25?

Server : No 27.

Back waiter : Ok got it.

Server : Thanks.

Exercise : Listening

Listen and fill in the blanks.

Server : Good afternoon ladies would you like ____ ________ ______________?

Guest 1 : _________sound wonderful.

Guest 2 : I'll have the same.

Server : Ok great are you ready to order, or do _____need more _____?

Guest 1 : I think were ready now I would like the ________ ________________________

Server : Ok the turkey and avocado sandwich, what would like on the side? We offer __________ _________, _________ _________or potato salad

Guest 1 : Could ___________________________?

Server : Of course

Guest 2 : I'll have the ___________.

Server : Ok madam one burger ______ _____ _______ _______ with that?

Guest 2 : That sounds wonderful.

Server : Ok then that's two ______ ______ and one ______ ______ ______ with pasta salad and one ________ ______ ______. Anything else?

Guest 2 : That sound right.

Server : Ok. Then I'll be ______________ with you food and drinks.

12 Chapter

Bar Service

Vocabulary

- desert wine
- blended
- shaker
- tray passed
- rocks
- well
- call
- premium
- straight up
- black russian
- cosmopolitan
- martini / dirty
- non-alcoholic
- on tap

Exercise

Match each question with appropriate response.

1. Would you care for a drink, sir?

2. What can I get for you to drink, sir?

3. Can you change this ten dollar bill?

4. Would you like it straight or on the rocks?

A. Certainly, sir.

B. A large scotch, please.

C. Yes, I'll have a black Russian.

D. Straight up, please.

Dialogue

(B/T : Bartender G : Guest)

B/T : hi, What are we having tonight?

Guest 1 : What do you have on tap?

B/T : We have bud miller and Samuel Adams.

Guest 1 : Uh, a bud sounds good.

Guest 2 : And ill have a dirty vodka martini.

B/T : Ok, coming right up.

Exercise : Speaking Activities

A. Make sentences out of the word below.

1. Would / a drink / care for / you / sir?

2. Yes, I'll / a black Russian / have

3. Would / straight up / like / it / you / or on the rocks?

4. What / to drink / I / for you / get / can / sir?

B. Fill in the information in the chart for yourself.

Then work in groups of four.

Ask the other students and fill in the information.

Question	Yourself	A	B	C
Would you care for a drink, sir?				

Bartender Service

(B/T : Bartender G : Guest)

G : Hello, Mr. Kim. Nice to see you again. I got here about an hour ago. How is everything?

B/T : Everything is just fine, sir. Would you care for a drink?

G : Yes. Fix me a martini and make it a dry one.

B/T : Very well, sir.

G : Bartender, Bring another round for us, please.

B/T : Another round of the same, sir?

G : Manhattan for me and gin and tonic for the lady.

Selling wine at the table

(G : Guest W : Waiter)

W : Would you like to see the wine list.

G : Yes please.

G : I'm in the mood for a nice red wine what would you suggest?

W : The Rothschild Cabernet Sauvignon really nice but if you're in the mood for a nice table wine I would suggest the Pinot Noir.

G : The Pinot sounds nice to me.

W : Excellent sir ill be right back with your bottle.

W : (waiter presents the bottle corks it and pours a small amount at the host glass and waits for the host approval)

G : Oh that will do very nicely.

W : Very good sir.(waiter now pours for the rest of the table)

Quick service

Once you have their order, serve them quickly. Prompt cocktail service is always appreciated.

Suggestive selling

A good waiter or waitress practices suggestive selling throughout the meal.

Example

G : Two New York steaks, one rare and one medium, please.

W : A bottle of Burgundy would go very well with your steaks, sir.

G : That's an excellent idea.

Certain wines go with different foods.

□ **Red wines :**

go well with hearty foods such as steak, roast duck, roast beef or pork chops.

□ **White wines :**

go well with light foods such as fish, seafood, and light meats like veal, chicken, or turkey.

□ **Champagne :**

can be served with everything. However, if the guest requests white wine with the steak, let him have it.

Serving temperature

□ **Red wines :**

should be served at room temperature (65°F).

To further enhance the flavor, they are sometimes opened a short time before they are served.

□ **White wines :**

All the white wines and sparkling wines are served chilled. More delicate flavor of these wines are enhanced by chilling.

Serving procedures

(1) Present a bottle of wine for the host's approval.

(2) Cut the cap.

(3) Insert the corkscrew well into the cork, with the bottle set firmly on the table.

(4) Pull the cork out smoothly and evenly.

(5) Wipe the lip of the bottle to remove any deposits that might affect the wine's taste.

(6) Pour a sip of wine and stop, allowing the host to taste it, and get his approval.

(7) Beginning with the guest on the host's right side, serve each guest 2 / 3rds of the glass, leaving an air-space at the top of the glass to hold the wine's aroma.

(8) Make a twisting action at the end of the pour. This is the secret to prevent dripping.

Opening champagne

Opening champagne can be a problem for the inexperienced waiter.

(1) Present the bottle to the host, and then place it back in the bucket.

(2) Keep your finger or thumb on top of the cork while removing the wire hood. That is to keep the cork from popping too soon and causing injury or embarrassment to your guests.

(3) Hold the cork firmly using a linen napkin in one hand and the bottle in the other. Twist the cork and the bottle in opposite directions. And let the pressure in the bottle push the cork into your hand. Champagne. When opened correctly. Emits very little sound and the cork never flies.

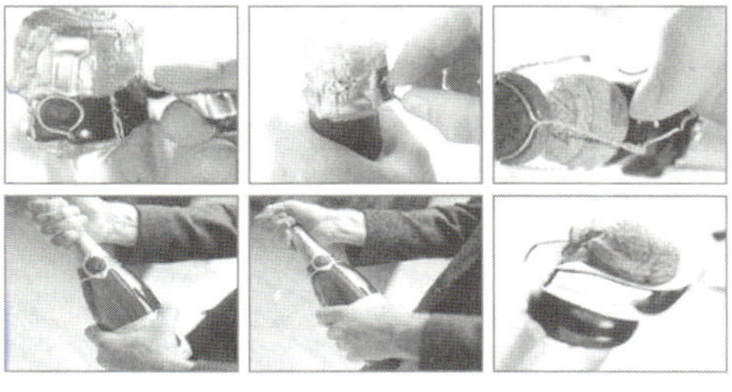

Selling Wine And Liquor

Whatever you're past experience as a waiter or waitress, you can learn a few basic principles about wine and liquor service that will make your job easier and more enjoyable.

You can learn :

A) How to suggest the appropriate wine for your guests entre.
B) How to make a make a suggestion for before-dinner drinks that will increase sales.
C) The basic procedures for opening and serving wines.

Exercise : Listening

Listen and fill in the blanks.

B : Good evening, sir. ______________________________ to drink?

G : A _________, please.

B : ___ __________, sir?

G : No, thanks. Just a little water, please.

B : Anything else, sir?

G : Yes. Would you Bring me a _______ _______ for my wife?

B : We have _______ ____ _______. What will she have?

G : _________ please, and where can I buy cigarettes?

B : There is a vending machine over there, sir.

G : OK. Can you _______________ dollar bill?

B : Certainly, sir.

Utensils For Cocktail-Making

1. Corkscrew 2. Can opener 3. Mixing glass 4. Shaker 5. Water pitcher 6. Bar-strainer with coil 7. Jigger 8. Ice bucket 9. Pint glasses 10. Champagne flute 11. Bucket glass	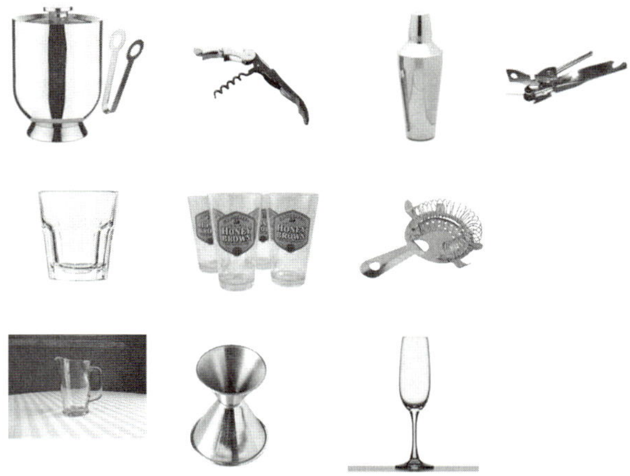

Listening Script

Chapter 1

A : SEOUL Airlines. May I help you?

P : Yes. I'd like to change my flight schedule.

A : May I have your name?

P : James Chastain. And my reservation number is 350-3500.

A : Thank you, Mr. Chastain.
Your reservation is Flight 026 going to New York.
How would you like to change it?

P : I'd like to take an afternoon flight.

A : Let me check if there are any afternoon flights.
Just a moment, please.

P : All right.

A : OK. We have some seats at 7 p.m.

P : Sounds great. I'll take it. Book me for the 7 p.m. flight, please.

A : All right, Mr. Chastain.

Your flight has been changed from flight 026 to 028, leaving Incheon at 7 p.m. and arriving in New York is at 8 p.m.

P : Thank you so much.

A : You're quite welcome. Thank you for flying SEOUL Airlines.

Chapter 2

A : Good morning. May I have your ticket and passport, please?

P : I have an e-ticket.

A : All right. I can find you on the computer.
Would you like an aisle seat or window seat?

P : Can I be assigned a seat by the emergency exit please?

A : Yes, sir. But you may be asked to assist our crew members in the case of an emergency.

P : No problem.

A : All right. Do you have any baggage to check?

P : Just one.

A : Could you put your baggage on the scale, please?

P : Sure.

A : Here are your boarding pass and baggage claim check. Your seat is 28C and the boarding gate is 15. Boarding will begin at 9:30 a.m. Have a pleasant flight.

Chapter 3

P1 : Excuse me, I think this is my seat.

F : May I see your boarding pass, please?
Thank you.
(to P2) Excuse me, ma'am.
May I see your boarding pass, please?
Thank you, ma'am.
(to P2) I'm sorry but I'm afraid you are in the wrong seat.
Your seat is right behind this one.

P2 : All right. I'm sorry.

F : (to P2) No problem. May I help you with your bag?

P2 : No, thank you.

F : (to P1) Thank you for waiting, sir. Here you are.

Chapter 4

F : Would you like to use a bassinet for your baby?

P : I would be glad to.

F : I'll be back to set up a bassinet for your baby after take-off.

P : Thanks. Do you have any baby items such as diapers?

F : Yes, we do, ma'am.
We have diapers, baby food, baby formula and bottles.
If you need anything for your baby, please let me know.

P : All right. Thank you so much.

F : Excuse me, ma'am.
Would you please hold your baby outside your seatbelt?
That will be more comfortable and safer for the baby.

P : Oh, I see.

(After take-off)

F : Excuse me, ma'am.

Would you like me to set up a bassinet for you?

P : Yes, that'll be helpful.

F : There you are. The bassinet is ready.

P : Thank you very much.

F : My pleasure. Have a nice flight.

Chapter 5

P : I'll have a Peach Coco.

F : I'm afraid I don't know that drink. Could you tell me how it's made?

P : It is made of orange juice, rum and peach tree.

F : I'm sorry, sir. But we don't have peach tree on board.
Would you like something else, instead?

P : What do you recommend?

F : May I suggest you try Bourbon & Coke?

P : I'll try that.

F : Here you are. I hope you enjoy it.

P : Thank you very much.

F : Would you like anything else?

P : Yes. Can I have more peanuts?

F : Certainly sir. Here you are.

Chapter 6

F : Excuse me, ma'am. Are you a U.S citizen or a resident?

P : Yes, I'm a U.S citizen.

F : Then you don't need this entry card, but you must fill out the customs form.

Chapter 7

F : Excuse me, sir.

We've not reached the parking area yet.

Would you please remain seated until the plane comes to a complete stop?

P : Alight.

F : Thank you.

Chapter 8

1. Of course. We offer turn down service as well as a pickup service from the airport free of charge.

2. I'm sorry, sir. We are fully booked. I can contact another hotel and see if they have any rooms available.

3. Can I get a 6:30 a.m. wake up call?

4. Seoul has a number of tourist attractions checks with Concierge see what other services are available.

5. I need any suit pressed. Do you offer a laundry service?

6. Hi. Is this room service I would like a hamburger and fries sent to room 301 please.

7. Well a double room is fine but if you really want comfort I would suggest the presidential suite.

8. I'm sorry we don't have a suite left but I can offer a wonderful double room with two beds.

9. Your room is 406 here is your key card would you like a wake up call?

10. There is a service charge of 10% for groups of ten or more.

Chapter 9

A) Good evening, room service. How can I help you?

B) Yes, I would like the valentines' dinner for two, sent to my room.

A) Ok, sir. How would you like the fillet cooked?

B) Medium rare, please and could also send a dozen red roses with that.

A) Ok, sir. Valentine's Day special for two and a dozen red roses, anything to drink.

B) What red wine do you suggest?

A) We have a wonderful house burgundy that goes great with the beef.

B) Ok, that sounds great.

A) Ok. that a Valentine's Day special one house burgundy and a dozen red roses, would like us to change your room?

B) That would be great.

A) What room shall I send it to?

B) I'm in 1503.

A) Very well sir. Have a wonderful evening.

Chapter 10

S : May I help you, sir?

C : Yes, please. I want to take a look at the gift shop. I need to find something for my kids.

S : That would be on the third floor next the escalator ; they have a wonderful selection of toys and gifts for kids.

C : Where is the escalator?

S : Just ahead. Right past the information booth on the left.

C : Thank you.

Chapter 11

Server : Good afternoon ladies would you like something to drink?

Guest 1 : Ice tea sound wonderful.

Guest 2 : I'll have the same.

Server : Ok great are you ready to order, or do you need more time?

Guest 1 : I think were ready now I would like the turkey and avocado sandwich.

Server : Ok the turkey and avocado sandwich, what would like on the side? We offer French fries, pasta salad or potato salad.

Guest 1 : Could I have the pasta?

Server : Of course.

Guest 2 : I'll have the hamburger.

Server : Ok madam one burger would you like fries with that?

Guest 2 : That sounds wonderful.

Server : Ok then that's two ice teas and one turkey avocado sandwich with pasta salad and one burger with fries. Anything else?

Guest 2 : That sounds right.

Server : Ok then ill be right back with you food and drinks.

Chapter 12

B : Good evening, sir. What can I get for you to drink?

G : A scotch, please.

B : On the rocks, sir?

G : No, thanks. Just a little water, please.

B : Anything else, sir?

G : Yes. Would you bring me a white wine for my wife? She's driving.

B : We have chardonnay or Chablis. What will she have?

G : Chardonnay, please, and where can I buy cigarettes?

B : There is a vending machine over there, sir.

G : OK. Can you change this twenty-dollar bill?

B : Certainly, sir.

Appendix

Chapter 1

Reserve / reservation
항공편을 이용하기 위한 예약

Airline
항공사

Flight number
항공편 명

Round trip
왕복편, 왕복여행

Inbound / outbound
임의의 도시 또는 공항을 기점으로, 들어오는 비행편과 나가는 비행편을 일컫는 용어

Ticket
항공권

Coach class
미국 국내항공에서 쓰이는 용어로 이등석. 즉 일반석, 이코노미석을 일컫는다.

Schedule
운항계획(시간표)

Stopover
여객이 적정 운임을 지불하여 출발지와 종착지 간의 중간지점에서 24시간 이상 체류하는 것을 의미하며, 요금 종류에 따라 도중 체류가 불가능한 경우가 있다.

Overbooking

특정 비행편에 판매가능 좌석수보다 예약자의 수가 더 많은 상태.
즉 No-Show 승객으로 인한 Seat Loss를 방지하여 수입제고를 도모하며 고객의 예약기회 확대를 통한 예약서비스 증대를 위해 실제 항공기 좌석 숫자보다 예약을 초과하여 받는 것을 말한다.

Confirm / reconfirm

주로 예약을 확인하는 것을 의미한다.(reconfirm은 예약을 재확인하는 것)

Address

5자리 혹은 6자리로 구성된 항공예약코드

Chapter 2

Check-in

탑승수속. 승객이 항공사 카운터에서 항공권, 여권, 비자 및 위탁수하물에 대한 수속을 하고 탑승권을 받기까지의 수속과정

Carry-on baggage

기내 반입 수하물(휴대품)

Checked baggage

승객이 화물로 부치는 탁송 수하물

Excess baggage

무료 수하물량을 초과하는 짐

Extra charge

무료 수하물량을 초과할 경우 부과되는 초과요금

Fragile

깨지기 쉬운(물품)

Baggage allowance

여객운임 이외에 별도의 요금 없이 운송할 수 있는 수하물의 허용량

Baggage claim tag

위탁수하물의 식별을 위해 항공회사가 발행하는 수하물 증표

Boarding pass

탑승권

Window seat
창측 좌석

Aisle seat
복도측 좌석

Unaccompanied child (minor)
성인의 동반 없이 혼자 여행하는 최초여행일 기준 5세 이상, 12세 미만의 유아나 소아

Passport
여권

Customs, immigration, quarantine
통상 CIQ라고 칭하며, 이는 Customs(세관검사), Immigration(출입국수속), Quarantine(검역)의 첫 문자로 정부기관에 의한 출입국 절차에 심사를 의미한다.

Transfer
여정상의 중간지점에서 여객이나 화물이 특정 항공사의 비행편으로부터 동일 항공사의 다른 비행편이나 타항공사의 비행편으로 바꿔 타거나 전달되는 것.

Delay / hold-up
비행기의 출발, 도착이 지연되는 것.

Chapter 3

Aboard
(비행기에) 탑승한

Boarding pass
탑승권

Front
(객실) 전방

Back
(객실) 후방

Aisle
통로, 복도

Empty seat
비어있는 좌석

Occupied
모두 탑승한 / 사용중인

Seating assignment
좌석배정

Upgrade
좌석승급

Seatbelt

좌석벨트

Overhead bin

객실 내 승객의 짐을 보관하는 승객 머리 위의 선반

Inconvenience

불편(사항)

Chapter 4

Turbulence
비행중 기류변화로 인한 기체요동

Coatroom
객실 내 승객의 옷이나 짐을 보관하는 공간

Valuable
귀중한(귀중품)

Emergency
비상사태

Window shades
객실 내 창문덮개

Bassinet
기내용의 유아요람으로 항공기 객실 내부 각 구역 앞의 벽면에 설치하여 사용한다.

Bulkhead seat
객실을 나누는 칸막이로 클래스(class)나 구역(zone) 사이에 설치된 분리 벽에 있는 좌석

Baby items
기내에 탑재되는 기저귀, 분유 등 아기용품

Captain
항공기 조종사, 기장

Cockpit
조종실

Departure time
출발시간

Destination
최종목적지

Lavatory
객실 내 화장실

Upright
직립의, 똑바로, 수직으로. 주로 '(등받이)를 바로 세우다'라는 의미로 활용된다.

Recline
'(좌석을) 뒤로 젖히다' 는 뜻.

Chapter 5

Refreshing
상쾌한

Careful
조심스러운

On board
탑승한, 탑재된

Tray table
기내에서 식기를 놓는 승객 개인 테이블

Chaser
'뒤쫓는 자' 라는 뜻으로, 독한 술 등을 직접 스트레이트로 마신 후 뒤따라 마시는 물 혹은 청량음료

Cocktail
일반적으로 알코올성 음료에 과즙류 혹은 비알코올성 음료 및 각종 향을 혼합하여 만드는 음료를 일컫는다.

Recommend
추천하다

Entrée
기내식 중 주요리

Run out of
다 소비되다

Heat up
음식을 데우다

Special meal
특별식

Kosher meal
유대정교 신봉자인 유태인 종교음식. 유대교 율법에 따라 조리된 음식으로 닭고기나 생선이 주가 되며, Bread 대신 Matzo라는 건빵이 쓰인다. 식기는 1회용 기물을 이용하고 종이상자에 봉해져 있으며, 서비스 준비 때 승객에게 반드시 허락을 득한 후 개봉하여 Heating해야 한다.

Entry card
입국 신고서(기록 카드)

Chapter 6

Disembarkation card
입국카드

Embarkation card
출국카드

Customs form
세관신고서

Quarantine form
검역신고서

Purser
객실사무장

Arrival time
도착시간

Declare
신고하다

Declaration form
신고서

Citizen / resident
시민권자 / 영주권자

Fill out / complete

(신고서를) 작성하다

Method of payment

지불방식

Chapter 7

Complimentary copy
무료로 제공하는(기내지)

Souvenir
기념품

Flying time
비행시간

Airsickness (bag)
비행기멀미

Chilly
추위를 느끼다

Dizzy
어지럼증을 느끼다

Upset stomach
속이 메스껍다

Sore throat
목이 아픈

Parking area
공항에서 여객의 승강, 화물의 적재 및 정비 등을 하기 위해 항공기가 주기하는 장소

Slippery
미끄러운

Watch your step
(계단 등을)조심하세요

Windy
바람이 부는

Wet
젖은

Chapter 8

Reservation
예약

Turn down service
고객이 투숙한 객실에 대하여 고객의 취침 직전에 제공하는 서비스로 간단한 객실의 청소, 정리, 정돈과 잠자리를 돌보아주는 서비스

Single
1인용 Bed를 설비한 객실

Double
2인용 Bed를 설비한 객실

Suite
'2실 이상의 연속 객실'이라는 뜻으로, 적어도 욕실이 딸린 침실 한 개와 거실 겸 응접실 한 개 등으로 짜여진 방을 의미한다.

Bell man
호텔 프런트에서부터 고객과 동반하여 고객의 짐을 운반하면서 객실까지 안내하는 직무의 종사원

Fully booked
전부 예약된

Concierge
도어키퍼(Door Keeper). 유럽풍 호텔에서 벨서비스 담당으로, 호텔에 관한 정보나 호텔 밖의 나이트 클럽, 레스토랑에 관한 정보, 극장표, 여행에 필요한 교통편, 안내 등의 포괄적 서비스를 제공한다. 이는 또한 서비스 감독자와 같은 뜻으로 고객 우편물 처리와 안내원, 도어맨 그리고 여행사와 손님의 관계에 관한 모든 업무를 총괄, 처리한다.

Pick up service
예약고객의 요청에 의해서 공항터미널에서 영접하여 호텔에 체크인시키는 서비스

Key card
키카드. 전자식으로 자물쇠를 열거나 기계 등을 조작하는 자기(磁氣)카드

Laundry service
호텔에 투숙 중인 고객의 세탁업무(물세탁서비스)

Wake up call
고객으로부터 아침 몇 시에 깨워달라는 부탁을 받고 교환원이 해당시간에 고객의 객실로 전화벨을 신호로 잠을 깨워 일어날 시간을 알리는 서비스

Room service
고객의 요청으로 음료, 식사 등을 호텔의 객실로 제공하는 식사서비스

Service charge
(계산서에 추가되는) 서비스 요금

Continental breakfast
계란요리를 곁들이지 않은 아침식사로 빵 종류, 주스, 커피나 홍차가 제공되는 조식

Chapter 9

Over easy-medium-hard

계란요리의 명칭으로 짧은 시간 조리하여 앞뒤를 다 익힌 것으로 속을 완전히 익히지 않을 것을 Over Easy, 중간 정도 익힌 것을 medium, 더 완전히 익힌 것을 hard라고 한다.

Omelet

계란요리의 하나로 흰자와 노른자를 섞은 후 프라이팬에 기름을 두르고 약한 불로 스크램블 식으로 휘저어 타원형으로 말아 제공하는 음식. 기호에 따라 속에 다양한 재료를 넣기도 한다.

Hash Browns

삶은 감자를 거칠게 다져서 양파, 베이컨, 소금, 후추, 파슬리를 넣고 튀긴 음식으로 주로 아침식사에 제공된다.

Brunch

아침 겸 점심의 겸용식사

Charge room

호텔 내에서 사용한 비용의 부담을 방비(room)에 부담하도록 하는 것

Cart

식당에서 음식을 나르는데 쓰는 네 발 달린 수레

Wrap

음식 등을 싸거나 포장하는 것

Caviar

소금에 절이고 press한 철갑상어의 알

Champagne

프랑스 샹파뉴지방에서 생산되는 발포성 와인

Espresso

이탈리아식 커피 추출법으로 농도를 진하게 추출해내는 방법

Appetizers

전채요리로 식사순서 중 제일 먼저 제공되어 식욕촉진을 돋구어 주는 소량의 요리를 말한다.

Poached

Lightly boiled된 요리형태로 원형을 상하게 하지 않은 채 뜨거운 물에서 삶은 것(주로 계란요리)

Chapter 10

Retail
소매(점)

Travel
여행

Compact / mid / full size
소형차 / 중형차 / 승합차

Mileage
마일리지

Gift
선물

Across from
~의 바로 맞은 편에

Next to
~의 바로 옆에

Intersection
교차로

Rotary
로터리 (회전식의), Roundabout

Chapter 11

Back waiter

Runner의 개념으로, 저장실에서 식음료를 식당에 운반하거나, 키친에서 테이블로 음식을 나르는 일을 하는 사람

Run

키친에서 테이블로 음식을 나르는 일

Window (also called the pass,)

음식을 손님에게 서비스하기 직전 Hot food를 뜨겁게 하기 위해 히팅 램프 아래에 놓는 것을 말한다.

Garnish

먹을 수 있는 식재료로 음식물을 보기 좋게 장식하는 것을 말한다.

Rare, Medium, Well

육류를 익힌 상태의 구분으로 Well done은 고기 속까지 완전히 익힌 것. Medium은 중심부가 모두 핑크빛으로 고기 절반만 익힌 것. Rare는 고기 겉만 익힌 것으로 붉은 날고기 상태를 말한다.

Hostess station / map

레스토랑 입구에서 좌석위치표 등을 놓고 안내하는 센터

Wait Station

분주한 식당 한 곳에 식사서비스 진행이 원활하도록 필요한 서비스물품들을 준비해 놓는 장소

Dressing

샐러드에 끼얹어 제공하는 것으로 샐러드의 맛을 한층 높여주는 역할을 한다.

10, 8, 2 Top
10명, 8명 또는 2명이 테이블에 앉았다는 것을 뜻한다.

Grilled
숯불이나 가스 혹은 전기복사열 같은 불꽃 위에 철판을 달군 석쇠에서 요리된

Specials
특별요리

Soup of the day
매일 바뀌는 요리사의 특선 soup

Dessert tray
식후 다양한 디저트류를 장식하여 준비한 트레이

Chapter 12

Dessert Wine
일반적으로 포트나 쉐리, 마데이라, 소테른 같은 단 맛이 나는 와인을 말한다.

Blended
두 개 이상의 성분을 철저히 믹싱하여 혼합하는 것

Call
name brand alcohol used in mixed drinks and for straight up drinks like jack Daniels on the rocks

Shaker
리큐르나 계란, 설탕 등 잘 섞이지 않는 재료를 잘 섞이게 함과 동시에 차갑게 하는 기구

Tray Passed
appetizers or drinks that are passed out by the waiter on a tray

Rocks
주로 유리잔에 얼음덩어리를 넣고 주류를 넣어 마시는 on the rocks의 용어

Well
Cheap alcohol usually used of mixed drinks (bourbon and coke)

Premium
The most expensive type of alcohol usually drunken straight
(grey goose vodka martini)

Straight up
알코올음료를 얼음과 함께 흔들거나 섞어서 걸러내거나, 얼음없이 글라스에 제공하는 방법

Black Russian

커피리큐어를 섞어 만드는 보드카 베이스의 칵테일. 제조는 일반적으로 보드카 1온스에 커피리큐어 0.5온스의 2대1 비율로 젓기법으로 만들며, 락글라스에 각얼음과 함께 제공한다.

Cosmopolitan

보드카 1온스, 꼬엥트로 0.5온스, 크랜베리주스 1온스, 라임주스 0.5온스를 쉐이크에 넣고 믹스하여 만드는 핑크빛 칵테일

Martini / dirty

Vodka에 dry vermouth를 섞은 후 올리브로 장식한 무색 투명한 칵테일 냄새는 향긋하지만 강한 쓴맛이 나며, 주로 식전에 마신다.

Non-alcoholic

알코올 성분이 들어있지 않은

On tap

일정 온도를 유지하며 언제든지 음료를 마실 수 있는 시스템으로 클럽이나 바에서 사용한다.

저자 소개

James Troy Chastain

Platt College of Design
  Bachelor of applied computer science
  Dual major: 3d Animation /Internet Design
Grosmont Comunity College
  Culinary Arts Certification
Suwon Science College
  Air Travel and Tourism Professor
Avalon
  English Teacher
Flinn Springs Inn
  Executive Chef
Bully's East
  Executive Sou's Chef
Rafters at spruce saddle
  Chef'De Cuisine
Briganteen
  Sou's Chef

Park Hye Jung

이화여자대학교 정치외교학과 졸업
세종대학교 관광대학원 관광경영학과 졸업 (경영학 석사)
세종대학교 대학원 호텔관광경영학과 졸업 (호텔관광학 박사)
대한항공 객실승무부 객실승무원
대한항공 객실훈련원 전임강사
동주대학 항공운항과 교수
현)수원과학대학 항공관광과 교수

Where Are You Going?

MP3CD포함

2011년 1월 15일 초판 인쇄
2011년 1월 20일 초판 발행

저자와의 합의하에 인지첩부 생략

저 자 James Troy Chastain
Park Hye Jung
발행인 (寅製) 진 욱 상
발행처 백산출판사
서울시 성북구 정릉3동 653-40
등록 : 1974. 1. 9. 제 1-72호
전화 : 914-1621, 917-6240
FAX : 912-4438
http://www.ibaeksan.kr
editbsp@naver.com

값 14,000원

ISBN 978-89-6183-415-5